MUD AN

C000138361

Contents

Stories illustrated by Pet Gotohda and Martin Chatterton

Heinemann

In this story

 Bones

 The master

 Wag

Tricky words

- bath
- scrubbed
- shook

Introduce these tricky words and help the reader when they come across them later!

Story starter

Bones is a big dog. Wag is a small dog. Bones is a very good dog but Wag is always getting into trouble. One day, Wag and Bones went for a walk but they got very muddy so the master said they needed a bath.

The Bath

"You need a bath,"
said the master.

Bones got in the bath.

The master scrubbed Bones.

He scrubbed and scrubbed.

Bones got out of the bath.

He gave Bones a bone.

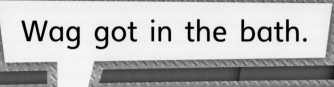

Wag got in the bath.

The master scrubbed Wag.

He scrubbed and scrubbed and scrubbed.

He got Wag out of the bath.

"Good dog, Wag,"
said his master.

10

Wag shook and shook
and shook.

"Bad dog, Wag," said his master.

Quiz

Text Detective

- What did the master do to Bones?
- Why was the master cross with Wag?
- Would you have been cross with Wag?

Word Detective

Phonic Assessment: Final phonemes

- Listen to the word 'need'. What phoneme can you hear at the end? Write the letter.
- Listen to the word 'out'. What phoneme can you hear at the end? Write the letter.
- Listen to the word 'dog'. What phoneme can you hear at the end? Write the letter.

Super Speller

Can you spell these words from memory?

bad   got   and

HA! HA! HA!

Q What has hands but never washes its face?

 A A clock.

In this story

 Silly Sid

Tricky words

- put
- eggs
- bowl
- break
- beat
- flour

Introduce these tricky words and help the reader when they come across them later!

Story starter

Silly Sid is a bit silly. One day, he decided to make a cake. He got out a recipe book and began to read it. The recipe book said, 'Put the eggs in the bowl.'

Silly Sid Makes a Cake

"I must put the eggs in the bowl," said Silly Sid.

Silly Sid put the eggs
in the bowl.

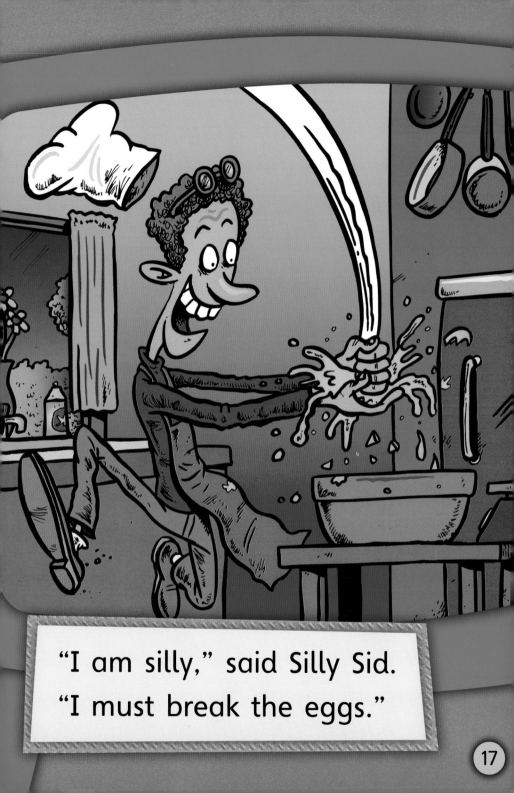

"I am silly," said Silly Sid.
"I must break the eggs."

"Now I must beat the eggs," said Silly Sid.

Silly Sid beat the eggs.

"I am silly," said Silly Sid. "That is not the way to beat the eggs."

"Now I must put the flour in the bowl," said Silly Sid.

Silly Sid put the flour in the bowl.

"Now I am not so silly,"
said Silly Sid.

Quiz

Text Detective

- What silly thing does Silly Sid do with the eggs?
- Is Silly Sid silly at the end of the story? How is he silly?
- Would you eat a cake made by Silly Sid? Why or why not?

Word Detective

Phonic Assessment: Final phonemes

- Listen to the word 'bowl'. What phoneme can you hear at the end? Write the letter.
- Listen to the word 'am'. What phoneme can you hear at the end? Write the letter.
- Listen to the word 'eggs'. What phoneme can you hear at the end? Write the letter.

Super Speller

Can you spell these words from memory?

not   the   now

HA! HA! HA!

Q Waiter, waiter, this egg is bad!

A Don't blame me sir, I only laid the table.

24